The Ultimate
Alphabet

THE ULTIMATE
· ALPHABET ·

MIKE WILKS

AN OWL BOOK

HENRY HOLT AND COMPANY
New York

C is for Carol and so is this book

Published in the United States by Henry Holt and Company, Inc.,
115 West 18th Street, New York, New York 10011.
Published in Canada by Fitzhenry & Whiteside Limited,
91 Granton Drive, Richmond Hill, Ontario L4B 2N5.

Library of Congress Cataloging-in-Publication Data
Wilks, Mike
The ultimate alphabet.
1. Wilks, Mike.   2. Alphabets in art.   3. English
language — Rhyme.   I. Title.
ND497.W638A4   1986   759.2   86-12111

ISBN 0-8050-0076-3
ISBN 0-8050-2516-2 (An Owl Book: pbk.)

Henry Holt books are available at special discounts
for bulk purchases for sales promotions, premiums,
fund-raising, or educational use. Special editions
or book excerpts can also be created to specification.
For details contact: Special Sales Director,
Henry Holt and Company, Inc., 115 West 18th Street,
New York, New York 10011.

First published in hardcover by
Henry Holt and Company, Inc., in 1986.

First Owl Book Edition — 1992

Designed by Bernard Higton
Printed and bound by Arnold Mondadori, Italy
Recognizing the importance of preserving the written word,
Henry Holt and Company, Inc., by policy, prints all of its
first editions on acid-free paper. ∞

3   5   7   9   10   8   6   4

1   3   5   7   9   10   8   6   4   2
pbk.

INTRODUCTION

Looking is not the same as seeing. We are all proficient at looking but very poor at *seeing*. Much of an artist's training is concerned with learning to see – or more correctly with *re*learning to see. Children have this ability from a very young age but inevitably the modern environment, the education system and the modes of communication that it utilizes soon reduce this priceless faculty to the level of merely being able to look at things. Some rare people retain this natural ability but most of us have it educated out of us from our time at school onwards. It is only through diligent training and after

many years of perseverance that the potential artist is able to see once more. People who study such things calculate that the average person in an art gallery will spend six seconds in front of each picture, and from my own observations I am sure that this is true. Just six seconds. If we merely look at a painting then I am surprised that it will hold our attention for this long, but if we *see* it then we might be lost within it forever. This then – the act of seeing – is what this book is all about.

For the last four years I have been on a journey. The place that I visited is not to be found in any atlas but it has proved to be unendingly fascinating and full of wonders, many of which were new to me and many which I delighted in rediscovering. This place is devoid of mountains, of valleys, deserts and lakes, it is not divided by tropics and meridians, and no oceans lap at its shore; yet we have each come to know the contours of this land in more intimate detail than the street outside our own front door. It is a continent which has been inhabited for centuries and within whose well-defined borders can be found the whole universe. My journey had twenty-six stops on the way where I paused to make a painting and tried to capture on canvas some of the spectacles that I found there. The name of this place is the English Language and in the pages that follow are to be found the pictures that I brought back with me from this grand tour. I hope that as you study these paintings and retrace my peregrination you will experience for yourself the pleasures of my visit and become as enriched by the journey as I know I have been.

Although I included a total of 8,050 words in these pictures, I suspect that the sharp-eyed will discover even more than those I consciously painted. In order to reap the rewards of my work you will need to do more than look at these reproductions – you will need to *see* them and, as I have stated previously, these two things are not synonymous. Here are some suggested ways of seeing, or if you like, of reading the pictures in order to help you extricate the words that you will find depicted there:

There are twenty-six pictures, one for each letter of the alphabet, and each illustrates a certain number of words. There may be as few as thirty items, as in the painting for the letter 'X', or as many as 1,234, as in the letter 'S'. Many of these words are common and without doubt already known to the average person, but some are more obscure and will require a little thought or research. The most valuable advice that I can convey is to look closely and to think about what you are looking at. Then if necessary look again and the answer may well reveal itself.

Always bear in mind that English is spoken in several countries and that objects are sometimes known by different names than the ones that you might be familiar with.

By far the largest number of words dealt with are the names of objects and parts of objects both animate and inanimate. Wherever possible I have used common names, which may change from country to country, although I have avoided dialect words. Sometimes things are commonly known by their technical or their Latin names like, for instance, all dinosaurs and some plants. In very rare instances some things have no common name at all, such as some species of fish or insect.

Some items will require you to name them with a single word like 'Catapult', some names are hyphenated like 'Ant-eater' and some will require more words to name them correctly like 'Grizzly Bear'.

Never overlook the obvious. Children, for reasons that I have mentioned before, are especially able to see things so obvious that they prove invisible to a more sophisticated eye and they will tend to notice such things as weather, shapes, colours and the initial letter itself.

To add to the fun of the pictures things are not always painted to scale and other things are often where you would not normally expect to find them.

Sometimes an image will depict something specific, sometimes something general and sometimes both at once. A bird you look at might be a blackbird, which would represent three words beginning with the letter 'B'—*bird, black* and *blackbird.* A snowman is made of snow and this image might represent two words, while the bird in the painting for the letter 'X' requires only a name beginning with this letter.

The appearance of more than one object in proximity to other similar objects might be significant although I have excluded words denoting position such as above, alongside, adjacent, abutting etc.

The overwhelming majority of the words depicted are current and modern although, please note, not all.

A symbol might have a name relevant to the picture that it appears in or it could stand for something beginning with a certain letter. A cross can also be seen as a plus sign (and even crosses, you will find, have a variety of shapes and names).

English is a magpie of a language and often appropriates to itself foreign words, incorporating them unaltered into its vocabulary. Its long association with French has supplied words like 'restaurant' and 'bouquet', while contact with other cultures means that we now use as our own such words as shampoo, pyjamas, pagoda and tycoon, all of which may, or may not, appear within the relevant pictures.

LOOK Only very few adjectives are to be taken into account.

Disparate objects sometimes share the same name and these should be identified separately. Therefore 'leg' (the support of a table or chair) and 'leg' (a bodily extremity) are defined as two entirely different objects and should be counted as such.

An object might have more than one name and that name might even begin with the same letter – snake and serpent for example.

One word derived from an image can sometimes indicate the presence of another. For example a juggler is juggling (two words) and a runner is running (again, two words).

Do not overlook the fact that these pictures are reproductions of works of art which also have their own family of words denoting artistic conventions, the most obvious being perhaps those of background and foreground.

Another thing that may prove fruitful if examined closely is my signature on each painting.

For many years I have also painted a snail into each of my pictures. My work, for obvious reasons, is apt to proceed slowly, so the inclusion of this creature seems singularly relevant and is put there to act on me as a goad when I revisit each work. In the case of this book its appearance in each painting is in some cases meaningful and in others not; you can be the judge. You might also notice that I have incorporated visual 'quotations' from works of art by other artists within these pictures. While the actual object that they represent is always in some way pertinent, the fact that they are there at all in that form is to be viewed as an act of homage on my part.

Most art forms rely on the skilful unravelling of time. You become a passive passenger on a long thin line that is stretched between 'once upon a time' and 'happily ever after', where the prospect is strictly limited to the small part of the world that the author wishes to reveal. Everything is frozen fast along this line of words, notes, film frames or whatever, in a strict and unalterable sequence. A picture, on the other hand, exists out of time. It is a country that we can wander through at will making our own pathways and discoveries, an endlessly fascinating terrain that surrenders its treasures to the observant and can be experienced anew at each visit. It requires an act of will to make this journey and you cannot be led by the hand as in other media. As in life, you yourself must make the effort to see.

Well, there you have an outline sketch of the terrain over which you are to travel, although I have provided a little more assistance for each specific letter which you will find on the pages facing each picture. In each case I have given the number of objects I consciously depicted.

This essay, which should not be seen as being in any way exhaustive, will be of help, but your own powers of observation will be your greatest aid. If I were to draw a map with too much detail I would run the risk of spoiling your own voyage of discovery.

I hope that you will find this journey as thrilling and as full of wonders and delights as I did.

Bon voyage!

The paintings that you will find reproduced in the pages of this book are the result of an idea that occurred to me several years ago. My original concept was to create a set of pictures, one for each letter of the alphabet, and to attempt to include in them images of *everything* known. I pursued this idea, and my researches indicated that even if I were to compromise over things such as the inclusion of every single variety of insect and make the canvases at least forty square feet it would still, with luck, take me twenty years to complete the task. This book as it now appears is a scaled down version of that original idea and was completed in four years almost to the day. It contains 8,050 items, although anyone with expertise in any particular subject will certainly be able to identify more in these images than I have intentionally included.

In creating each of these works, my first task was to compile a list of words for possible inclusion in the picture and then to ascertain just what each thing looked like. This might take up to three weeks. Next I produced a small rough pencil sketch to work out the composition, one of which is shown here, and is the seed from which the painting shown on the opposite page grew.

The next stage was to produce a plethora of accurate but very basic drawings on flimsy paper to the final size of the individual elements that would be incorporated in the painting. These were done from as many sources of reference as I could find, so as to make the image as typical of the object depicted as possible. These drawings, often little more than outlines, would later be traced through onto the canvas where as much as ninety-nine per cent of the work took place. This procedure would be repeated at intervals during the creation of the picture.

I then prepared a canvas with six coats of gesso – a brilliant white ground – carefully sandpapering each coat smooth between applications. All of the paintings were made with acrylic colours and I utilized a technique that would have been familiar to painters of the Renaissance more than 400 years ago. Here is a simplified example of the process.

I would start with underpainting and slowly build up in monochrome the form and shading of each image in this way. I used a warm neutral tone mixed from burnt umber and deep purple for the underpainting of warm colours, and a cool neutral of burnt umber and ultramarine for cool colours. Then with a sable brush I would begin applying thin transparent glazes of the final colour, each glaze being modified and carefully modulated as I progressed. There

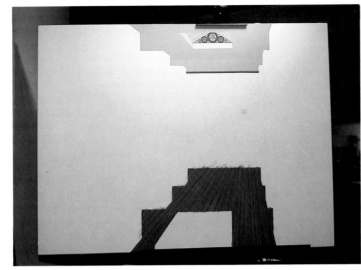

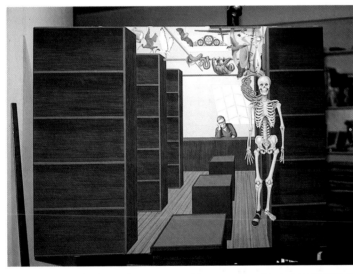

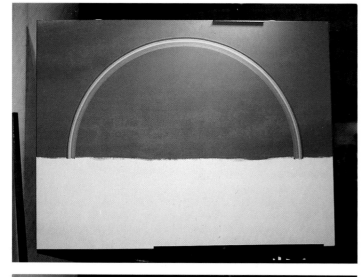

might be twenty or more such layers in any small area of the painting with the underpainting showing through. Such a process is of course slow and laborious and to speed the drying time of the colours I would often work with a paintbrush in one hand and a hair-dryer in the other blow-drying the paint as I proceeded. When the glazing of this local colour was complete I would glaze on the surface modulations of colour that can be observed on any object, and then tones such as reflected shadows, before finally applying highlights with opaque colour.

The brilliance of these colours relies on light being reflected from the white gesso ground back up to the eye through the coloured glazes. Naturally the composition needed to be carefully thought out and monitored as the painting progressed, and any afterthoughts or corrections necessitated a fresh white ground being laid on top of the existing painted surface before it was possible to recommence painting using this technique. To render the effect of distance, objects were overpainted directly onto the background colour, as the resulting loss of brilliance echoed the apparent effect caused by the atmosphere.

When working with very dark or opaque colours this glazing procedure would be modified and a mid-tone of local colour laid down with the darker modelling glazed on top. Semi-transparent lighter tones would then be meticulously glazed on and any highlights added as before. Wherever possible I deliberately avoided the use of black, the dark areas in any picture being created by the repeated application of deep coloured glazes which give a depth and luminosity that would otherwise be lacking. At the other end of the scale pure white was only used for the brightest highlights.

I also employed a whole range of techniques to create the appearance of texture. These ranged from the use of fingers and thumbs to balls of newspaper dipped in colour that could then be dragged across the surface of the canvas causing a semi-random texture. Often I used combinations of many such techniques.

Perhaps the only truly modern technique that I employed was the use of an airbrush – a small superfine spray-gun powered by compressed air – when applying large areas of colour that needed to be carefully gradated from light to dark.

The depiction of three-dimensional space on a two-dimensional surface is the great problem that lies at the heart of all representational painting and I employed several additional devices to help to create this illusion. If two objects were to appear closely separated in space then I painted a cast shadow, or to create the effect of greater spatial separation I might paint a subtle 'halo' around the foremost object. On rare occasions I used the common device of an outline to help to achieve this.

The original paintings were created in alphabetical order. The larger paintings measure 30″ x 40″ (76 cm x 102 cm) and the smaller works 30″ x 20″ (76 cm x 51 cm).

Some stages in the gestation of a painting can be witnessed from the photographs reproduced opposite. I spend between twelve and fourteen hours a day, seven days a week at my work, and a painting such as this would occupy me totally for four months.

The artist inhabits a strange world, an insubstantial world of shadows and essences, one whose boundaries are perhaps more permeable than normal. It is a secret realm where reality and illusion freely intermix and combine, often creating the eccentric, sometimes the haunting and rarely the marvellous. It can be a difficult and lonely existence, where long hours are spent striving after impossible goals and pursuing ideals that retreat faster than they can be approached. The image that I always carry of the artist is that of an illusionist. The auditorium is full of people and the illusionist is alone on the stage. He performs his act which has, by dint of years of diligent practise, been honed to what he hopes is some fine degree. If all proceeds as planned the audience is astounded and believes, if only fleetingly, that a marvel has happened there before their very eyes. It is the creation of this marvel for which I continue to strive.

I have painted 361 things beginning with the letter A
in this picture. Try and spot an amputee (he is also an
athlete although not animate), an abbey, an apricot,
an atlas (naming the oceans and continents that you find there),
an artilleryman and his ammunition, an aardvark, an
autogyro (why should it be upside down?), an ark full of
animals, an aerial paled by the distance, the
Egyptian god Annubis and a close colleague.
If you tip the page away from you at an acute angle
and, using only one eye, look along the anamorphic projection
to the right of the archangel, it will foreshorten
into a perfect ant.

B

Wander through this picture and attempt to find
a big building built from lots of Bs, a balustrade, a boomerang,
a booth complete with a buxom barmaid, various
buttons, badges, braids, bows and beads, a blond baby with a
baffling blemish on its bib, an ecclesiastical gentleman
having as much trouble seeing as the one immediately behind him,
and beds of more than one variety. I have
depicted 542 Bs altogether.

I have painted 436 things here. Look out for
a celibate catholic clergyman or cleric and his somewhat
relevant pet, a carved cryptogram and also a clue
to crack it with, a cliff bathed in crepuscular light, a
clarinetist and his clarinet, a camouflaged chameleon,
a cave or cavern complete with cracks and crevices, a crowing
cockatrice and a curious face on a clock that
needs to be thought about.

It is dawn in the desert and the dormant
decumbent deity needs a name. Also to be identified are a
donjon, a male mallard and his offspring, a diptych
full of delightful Ds, a dugong, a discobolus (without his
head for some reason), a dolmen, a diadem and dogs that
will reward close inspection. There are lots more to be spotted —
I painted 253 Ds in total.

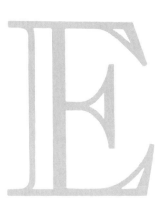

A visit to this exhibition full of enormous
exhibits will reveal that I have included 261 examples of items
beginning with the letter E. Somewhere there you will
find a blind Egyptian and an expanded one, an ensign, an enchained
escapologist, an escarpment, energetic volcanic activity, an
imperial man and an imperial bird, an ectomorph, an eel,
an emerald and a banana (why should this be there?).

Find if you can a firedrake and an apt adjective,
a flamingo, a flan, a farthingale and five famous flags.
There is a flying boat (with fixtures), a flying
fish, a flying lizard, a flying saucer and a piece of flying
architecture. There are more flights of fancy to find
and figures to fuss over. I painted 418 but you
may well finish up with more.

In a graveyard full of graven images
is to be found a Gypsy guitarist garbed in
gaudy garments which bear close examination.
Not so colourful are a gargoyle, a glengarry, a guillemot,
a galleon, a group of geese (mother, father and
children) and a classical knot. Try and identify
the 259 words I painted here.

Here are some helpful hints for the letter H.
There is a harpy and her eagle, a hill and its constituent parts,
a halberdier with a heraldic fish, a helping of 'halfs'
and 'hemis' and a male and female deer. Among the 277 Hs in this
picture you will find a highlander (dancing
his dance), edible and non edible dogs, a hamburger and a
well known hoaxer holding a hybrid.

I

If you identify all of the items I painted
in this picture you will have a list of 206 words. Included will
be an iguana (do not ignore his footmarks), an Irish
setter, an ironclad, an infantryman with an ingenious insignia,
various interesting inhabitants of an inn, an invalid near
a suitable location and many more icy items.

A juggler is juggling a jumble of Js.
This jungle of images also includes a juvenile,
a suitably clad jockey and a jester.
Fill in the missing pieces – there are 102 things
in all and puzzle out this picture.

Three kinds of king, a knight or two,
a kite or two, a hole for knees and a hole for keys,
a krill and a grampus escaped from the letter G.
105 Ks for you to find and name.

L

Look closely and you will see among the
278 words depicted here a llama and a lama – the latter
is happy because he has his dog with him – a lackey
in livery making light work of his task, a lad with a
ladle in foreign garb, several different kinds of
line, several different kinds of lock, a family of lions
and the world's worst life-preserver.

M

I intentionally painted 410 words into this picture.
There is a multitude of mammals on the midway including a monk,
a minstrel appropriately dressed but recently bereaved,
a mountie and a monarch with attractive regalia. There are
mythical creatures as well – a reflective mermaid,
a manticore and a muscular minotaur in chains. There is a musketeer
with the tools of his trade, a marionette, a mullion and
somewhere a (deliberate) mistake.

Find the numbers nine, nineteen and ninety
twice over and name the constituents of the nosegay.
There is also a nun, a nurse and a starry
god of the deep among the 163 things in this nocturne.

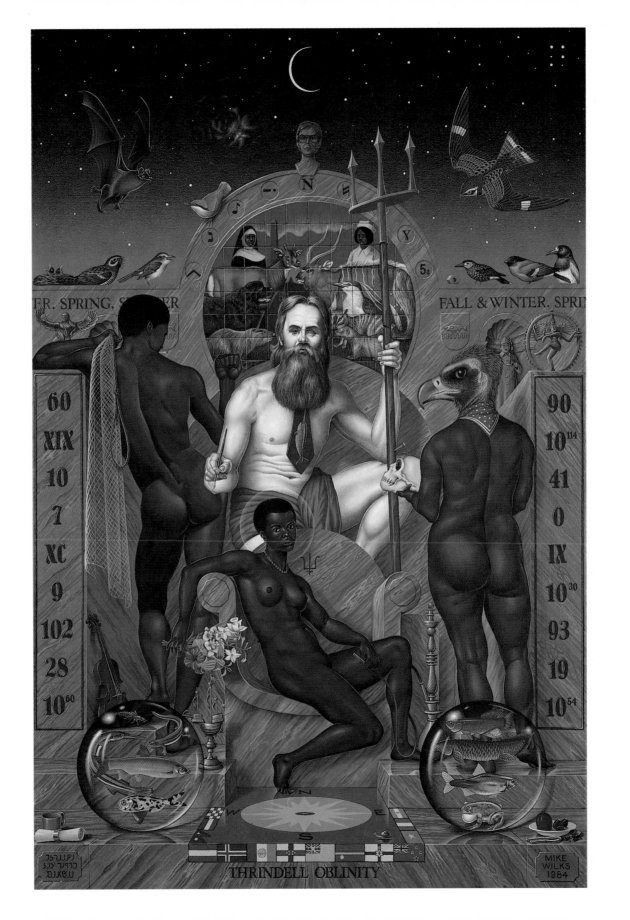

THRINDELL OBLINITY

Observe the buildings overlooking the ocean
and also look for an owl, an ostrich, an ox, an okapi, an
orang-utan and an ounce that weighs many a pound.
There are two musicians — an oboist from the east and an
organist from the west. The observant will find
my 161 Os in this picture.

A picture of pictures. Portrayed here you can find a
painter in profile clad in Ps whose palette is charged with
appropriate colours, a patchwork quilt of pertinent
hues, a pineapple, a pestle, a press and some proofs (can you
place the image?), a partially painted panda, a plethora
of pargeting in appropriate material, a paperback publication
and plenty of patterns for you to put into perspective.
Perspicacious persons may peceive more than the
810 Ps that I painted on purpose.

SUBI DURA A RUDIBUS.

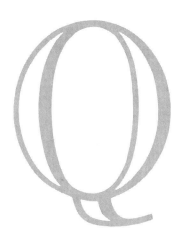

The picture on the opposite page has 309 or more Qs
painted in it. There is a quartet, a quartet, a quartet
and a quartet. A quail, a quail, a quail and
a quail. A quaker, a quaker, a quaker and a quaker.
And a quarry or two or three or four.

R

Within the ruins pictured on the right you can
recognize a rider on a rearing horse that did not win the
race, a rickshaw, a rocket, a rotunda, a religieuse
who might experience inspirational difficulties, a rebec, a rodent
and a rose or two. This reproduction needs to be read
carefully to reveal all. Your total could well run beyond
the 324 I consciously rendered.

The shelves of this store are stacked with stock.
You will find a steamship, a sailing ship and even a spaceship.
There are several sorts of shoe and scores of signs and
symbols. There is a sketch of a squinch, a selection of shells
(not all from the sea), a siamang settled on a seat, a
sponge to be studied and sundry stuff suspended from strings.
In all I included 1,234 Ss for you to see.

This painting is teeming with 430 Ts.
There is a teapot, a teacup, a T-square and a T-shirt.
There is a tortoise and members of his family, a tuba, a trombone,
a trumpet and an unrelated practitioner of this instrument.
There is also a set of literary twins, a telephone and a tractor
towing a trailer. There are enough trees to
traumatize any topiarist.

Uncover all of the Us in this picture
and you will have 133 more words.
There are some ums, lots of uns and ups and
some urs among others.

Clearly visible in the painting on the
right hand page are a vizsla, a violin, a viola, a vice,
a couple of vampires, a couple of vexillological
virgins and volumes more Vs to be verified. There are probably
more than the 149 than I have counted.

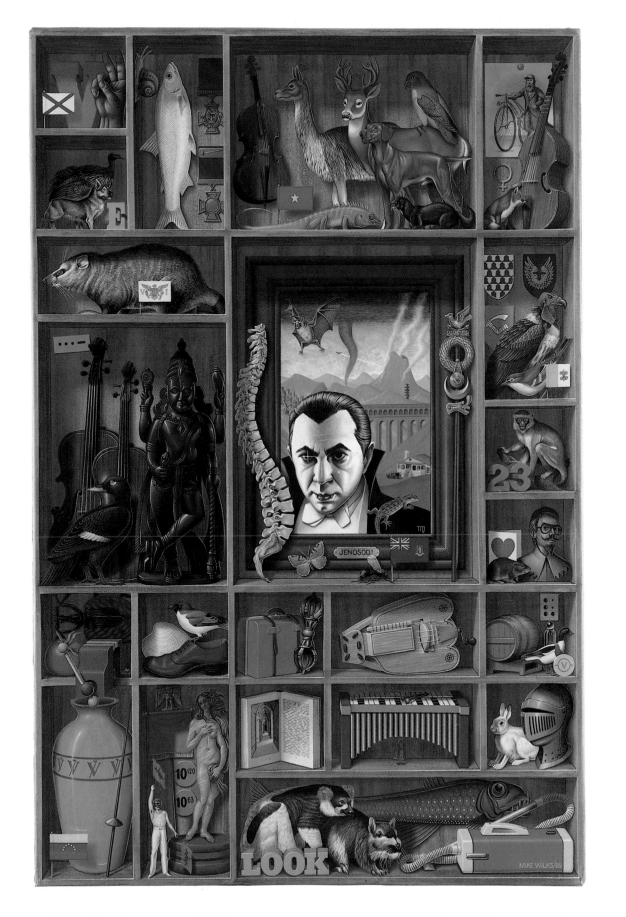

This is the picture for the letter W.
If you are watchful and wide awake you may well see
a witch with a wand and a walking-stick somehow attractive
to the bird that is clinging to it. There is a whiskered
wizard engaged in a literary pursuit, a wombat, a warming pan
and an alcoholic beverage of an appropriate colour
in an appropriate vessel. I depicted 268 words within this work.

A xylophone, its player and the 25th of December account
for 10 per cent of the words in this picture.

Mike Wilks 1985

The names of all of the birds, all of the
fish and all of the insects begin with the word yellow.
All in all there are 74 Ys for you to find
in this penultimate painting.

This is the ultimate picture in this book
and there are only 57 more steps remaining for you to
complete this journey. Can you find a zebra,
a zeppelin, a zebu, a zither, an African from the south and
one from the north? How many have you scored?

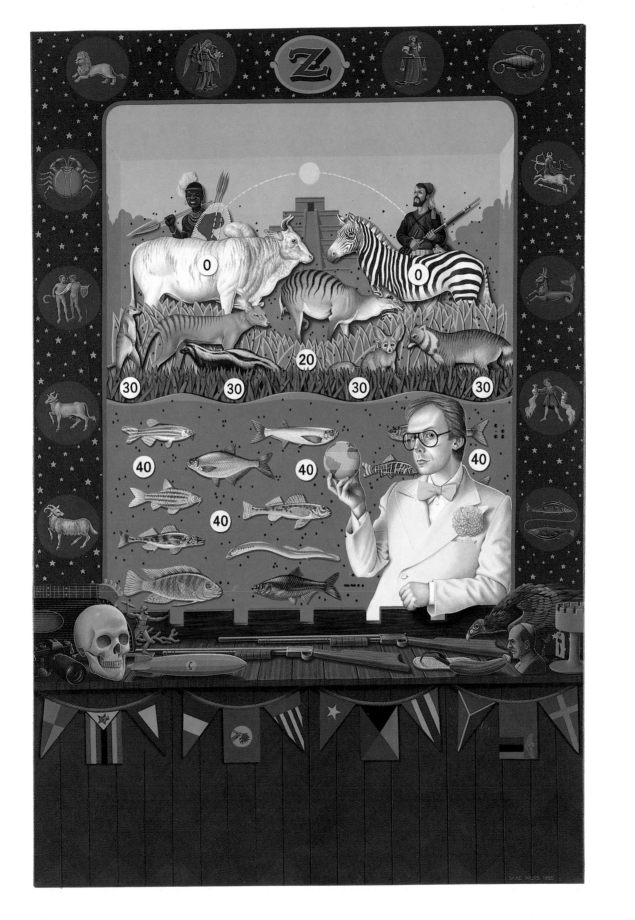

AFTERWORD

This is the book that changed my life. In retrospect it is evident that I achieved with it what I set out to do – that is, to make people look at my pictures. And how they looked! Even today, more than six years after the book was first published, I am still receiving congratulatory letters from fascinated Ultimate Alphabeteers from all over the world. I am surprised and more than a little delighted at how hard they have looked too. In 1988 I published *The Annotated Ultimate Alphabet* with, what I thought at the time, the definitive list of the words to be found in the paintings, but people are constantly finding many more words in the images than even I thought were there. In that respect, *The Ultimate Alphabet* has acquired a life of its own and I am certain that people will continue to find new words in these images for many years to come.

And how the world has changed in those same six years. The Soviet Union, once the largest country in the world, has ceased to exist, Germany is now referred to in the singular and a plethora of new countries that I only knew from out-of-date atlases of my childhood have been reborn. I have not attempted to update the canvases to reflect this for it would be a very naïve person who predicts that the world will remain as it is today. In the same spirit I have not added to the total number of words that I *consciously* included in each picture. Look upon these figures as the minimum number of words depicted. See if you can find more – I am sure you can.

Autumn 1992